CHARLES ST

First published in 2000 by
Mercier Press
PO Box 5 5 French Church St Cork
Tel: (021) 275040; Fax: (021) 274969; e.mail: books@mercier.ie
16 Hume Street Dublin 2
Tel: (01) 661 5299; Fax: (01) 661 8583; e.mail: books@marino.ie

Trade enquiries to CMD Distribution 55A Spruce Avenue
Stillorgan Industrial Park Blackrock County Dublin
Tel: (01) 294 2556; Fax: (01) 294 2564
e.mail: cmd@columba.ie

ISBN 1 85635 302 8
10 9 8 7 6 5 4 3 2 1

Cover design by Penhouse Design
Printed in Ireland by ColourBooks Baldoyle Dublin 13

CHARLES STEWART PARNELL

SEAN McMAHON

MERCIER PRESS

CONTENTS

CHRONOLOGY

1846   Born in Avondale, County Wicklow, on 27 June

1869   Rusticated from Magdalene College

1875   Returned as MP for Meath

1877   Begins a policy of obstruction in Parliament, an extension of the technique devised by Joseph Biggar

1879   President of Irish National Land League

1880   On tour in America with John Dillon; hurries home to fight in the general election, returned for Cork, Mayo and Meath; meets Katharine O'Shea, the estranged wife of Captain O'Shea; famous 'leper of old' speech at Ennis;

prosecuted with other leaders of Land League but jury is split

1881   Coercion act offset by Land Law (Ireland) Act, granting the 'Three "F"s': fair rent, fixed tenure, free sale; arrested and imprisoned in Kilmainham; Land League suppressed

1882   Mrs O'Shea has Parnell's first child; 'Kilmainham Treaty' and release of Land League leaders; Phoenix Park murders

1885   Parnellites, with 86 seats, hold balance of power between Conservatives (249) and Liberals (335); 'Hawarden Kite' indicates Gladstone's growing commitment to Home Rule

1886   Parnell insists that O'Shea be candidate in Galway;
        Gladstone introduces first Home Rule Bill, which
        will reserve main powers to Westminster
        (defeated by forty votes on second reading); Parnell
        not in favour of O'Brien's Plan of Campaign

1887   The *Times* publishes defamatory articles on 'Parnell-
        ism and Crime'

1888   Conservative government establishes a commission
        which effectively puts the whole nationalist move-
        ment on trial

1889   Richard Piggott, the forger of the *Times* letters,
        admits forgery, commits suicide; Parnell visits
        Hawarden to work with Gladstone on a Home
        Rule settlement; O'Shea files for divorce,
        naming Parnell as co-respondent

1890   Irish Party splits after Room 15 debate, with a
        majority opposed to Parnell

1891   Marries Mrs O'Shea on 25 June; dies on 6 October

1

AVONDALE AND CAMBRIDGE

There have been three great Irish statesmen since the Act of Union of 1800: Daniel O'Connell (1775–1847), Charles Stewart Parnell (1846–91) and Éamon de Valera (1882–1975). All strove to have the act repealed and none quite succeeded, but each left an indelible mark on what was to become a modern constitutional democracy. All had elements of drama in their lives but only one would have interested Aristotle, in that his career had almost a classical Greek theme, with a tragic hero of palpable nobility who had a character defect which led to a cosmic mistake and his ultimate downfall. However, Parnell was also made the hero of a melodrama of the kind that was the stuff of the plays of his time – not that he ever frequented the theatre – and the cause of his downfall and death was, to the theatrically minded, 'that woman'. Given the romantic elements of the story, it is slightly odd that Hollywood did not make more of it: the 1937 film *Parnell*, with Clark Gable notably miscast as the Chief (as he was known) and Myrna Loy as Katharine, was a flop. The best representation of Parnell on the screen was in a cameo role played by Robert Donat in *Captain Boycott* (1947). The scene is based on an 18 September 1880 speech by Parnell in which he brilliantly adumbrated the technique of ostracism that was to prove so successful in the Land War.

In the Ireland of the 1940s, when the Church was at its most aggressively devotional, the jibing observation was made that Dublin's O'Connell Street had statues to three adulterers. This crack was probably true but unprovable about the 'huge-cloaked Liberator' at the lower end of the street – any transgressions he committed were discreet and certainly casual; there was no doubt about Nelson, 'the one-handled adulterer' in the middle, since Emma Hamilton was his constant dry-land companion; and Parnell, at the top, certainly lived with another man's estranged wife and died in her arms. Though Katharine O'Shea was a character in the media-induced melodrama, she was merely a catalyst in Parnell's Sophoclean tragedy. The determinants of the graph of his life were his remarkably enigmatic character and his probably unconscious arrogance, which amounted to hubris. Biographers have offered a variety of diseases as the cause of his wretched appearance and chronic ill-health throughout the last decade of his life, but the most recent diagnosis, by J. B. Lyons in *What Did I Die Of?* (1991), suggests that the described symptoms are simply those of myocardial infarction – or heart attack, as your doctor would call it. Whatever about the reason for it, a heart attack was a fitting end to the tragedy.

The Parnells had been in Ireland since Charles II had appointed James Butler, Duke of Ormonde, viceroy in 1660. One member of the family, the Rev Thomas Parnell (1722–97), had been a friend of Jonathan Swift and Alexander Pope and the author of 'A Night-Piece of Death', which initiated a genre of graveyard verse and inspired Thomas Gray's 'Elegy'. Sir John Parnell (1744–1801), the Chief's great-grandfather, had been Chancellor of the Exchequer in Grattan's Parliament and a vigorous opponent of the Union (but was not otherwise noted for liberalism) and it was his son William (1777–1821), Parnell's grandfather, who had suggested to O'Connell the device of the 'Catholic Rent', which had a major psychological and financial impact on the agitation for Catholic Emancipation. His son John Henry (1811–59) led a quiet huntin', shootin', fishin', cricketin' life in his demesne at Avondale, near Rathdrum, County Wicklow, which had been the family home since 1777. He was unusual in only one respect: in 1835 he had married an American, Delia Tudor Stewart. Her father, Commodore Charles Stewart – 'Old Ironsides', master of the warship *USS Constitution* – had captured two British ships during the War of 1812 and it is believed that her influence upon her second son, who bore her name, was to question Britain's automatic right of domination in Ireland. She was no fiery revolutionary – her daughters were presented at court – but such topics as republicanism and tenants' rights were discussed. And when the son seemed to turn against his class he did not have to turn against his family.

Charles Stewart Parnell was born on 27 June 1846, the second son and seventh child of eleven. His surname was stressed on the first syllable, as in Yeats's lines, 'And Parnell loved his country/And Parnell loved his lass', but the ballads of the time and the modern usage prefer 'that horrible emphasis on the 'nell that is so prevalent', as his widow wrote in her book. The family had a poor health record: the grandfather was only forty-four and the father forty-eight when they died, probably of coronaries; these ages were rather below the life expectancy of their class. Fanny, Parnell's favourite sister, died suddenly in 1882 at the age of thirty-four and their sister Sophie was thirty-two when she died. Parnell had typhoid while at school in Yeovil, Somerset, but generally had a reputation for wiriness and physical endurance.

Parnell's interests were scientific rather than literary; unlike the men who were his political colleagues – T. P. O'Connor, Tim Healy and Justin McCarthy – he was not well-read nor could he write with any skill or grace. It took all the power of his will to overcome his lack of rhetorical skills and he never lost the fear of public speaking. From his boyhood he conducted scientific experiments and wasted a deal of money in trying to mine gold in County Wicklow. He had become the owner of Avondale at the age of thirteen, on his father's death – his father ignoring primogeniture and excluding his wife from the will. Delia had money from other sources, and John, the surviving elder brother, was given family land in Armagh and was known to be his uncle's heir. The children were made wards of Chancery, possibly to make sure that their mother did not whip them off to her home in Massachusetts. She did not like Avondale and let it to various tenants while she and the family lived in rented houses in Dublin. The family retained the dower house as a summer residence where the young landlord could play cricket and keep an eye on his property.

A youth of his class needed an education and after three years of private tuition he was sent to a crammer at Chipping Norton, Oxfordshire, to prepare him for entrance to

Magdalene College, Cambridge. His university years (1865–9) were undistinguished, the only event of much note being his rustication for drunkenness, brawling and trying to bribe a constable. The event was uncharacteristic and significant only in that Parnell, who was normally abstemious, revealed an innate pugnacity which rarely surfaced. He had shown very little interest in his studies, with the exception of mathematics, and though he had a few close friends he was not popular. He certainly felt ill at ease with most of the English undergraduates in what was then a very 'hearty' college. University life had given him his first understanding of the odd intermediate position that was the lot of the Anglo-Irish when out of Ireland. The condescending attitude of the natives, as he perceived it, nettled him and perhaps caused his reappraisal of his own political beliefs.

The rustication was imposed in May with only a week of term to go, so it could not be regarded as a very severe punishment. Even so, Parnell did not return to his college and went down without taking any degree. He had already taken charge of his property on his twenty-first birthday at the end of his second year at university and it suited the mood of the moment for him to be a benevolent squire. (He remained an indulgent landlord, as the accounts of the estate reveal; this trait meant that the estate and its lord were in constant financial difficulties.) The young master was tall, fair and regarded as very handsome, with notably impressive eyes. He spoke without a trace of an Irish accent and he should in the terms of the time have been quite a catch. He had flirted a little at parties at the time of his accession. One young lady, whom he nicknamed 'Mouse', had thought that his interest in her was more than passing but nothing came of the dalliance.

Much more serious was his pursuit in 1870 of a Miss Woods, a rich heiress from Rhode Island, whom he had met while staying with his mother in Paris. This Jamesian interlude was interrupted when, in the spring of 1871, she and her mother left suddenly for home while Parnell was in

Wicklow attending to estate business. He followed her across the Atlantic, using the excuse of a visit to his elder brother John, who was a successful peach-farmer in Alabama. He was received in the Woods's house in Newport with politeness but no acceptance. Miss Woods may have felt that a republican New Englander had too little in common with an Irish landlord who seemed to have no serious purpose in life. Parnell, who was deeply in love with her, took this rejection hard. He spent the rest of the year in America, partly with John and partly on a tour of coal and iron mines, looking for investment opportunities. As ever, his attitude to his own position was ambivalent; he felt that as an Irishman he ran the risk of being slighted by the Protestant Yankee grandees but he did not wish to be associated with the Irish of the diaspora, who, a quarter of a century after they had arrived as Famine refugees, were ceasing to be shanty Irish. He returned home in January 1872, little realising that these same Irish-Americans would play a significant part in the political career upon which he would soon embark.

2

PARLIAMENTARIANISM

The country to which he returned and which he regarded with the eye of a stirring politician was in a kind of ferment. William Ewart Gladstone (1809–98) had been Liberal prime minister for four years and had already begun to do what he could 'to pacify Ireland'. He had been a Conservative and a disciple of Sir Robert Peel (1788–1850) in his advocacy of free trade and after many years had found his niche as a pragmatic Liberal with a strong moral sense. Unlike his mentor, he had not had an adversary of the calibre or virulence of O'Connell and he bore no especial animus against the Catholic Irish. He had been profoundly stirred, as was Isaac Butt (1813–79), by the tragedy of the Famine and the activities of the Fenians, whose unsuccessful campaigns had been such a feature of the second half of the 1860s.

The idea of righting Ireland's wrongs by revolution had been kept alive by the heirs of Young Ireland and the abortive rising of William Smith O'Brien in 1848, and many Irish-Americans had learned military skills on both sides during the American Civil War. Any chance of a successful campaign in Ireland had been lost when the government had arrested the main leaders in 1865. (Though the movement had a wide base, with members in the RIC, prison staffs and the army, it was also riddled with informers.) The societies which grew out of it – the Irish Republican Brotherhood (IRB) in Europe and Clan na Gael in the US – though virtually inactive for many years, were to play a significant part in twentieth-century politics. The post-war forays into Canada were no more successful that the attempted rescue of two Fenian prisoners in Manchester in 1867; this incident led to the hanging of William O'Meara Allen, Michael Larkin and William O'Brien and their canonisation as the 'Manchester martyrs'. That event and the stories of ill-treatment of Fenian prisoners – O'Donovan

Rossa (1831–1915) was kept for weeks with his hands manacled behind his back – prompted a huge surge in support for the movement. Butt, who had defended the Fenians, was impressed by their earnestness and integrity and, arguing that the events of the Famine had proved that the Act of Union was a kind of fraud, became a non-violent supporter of the movement. An Amnesty Association was founded in 1869 with him as president and the following year he started the Home Government Association, which was the basis for Home Rule agitation.

Gladstone was alert to Irish public feeling and when he saw that a man like Butt, who had once been an arch-unionist, had been converted to the cause of repeal he responded; his mind was further focused by the Clerkenwell dynamiting, when, in another attempt to rescue Fenian prisoners, 30 people were killed and 120 seriously injured. With the usual republican logic, this event was taken to be the stimulus for Gladstone's mission and not the reason for its near-abandonment. (Parnell himself was to make the same noises several times on public platforms but for his own purposes.) The disestablishment of the Irish Church in 1869 and a land bill of 1870 that required that an evicted tenant be compensated for his improvements were taken as an indication of good intent on Gladstone's part but there was to be more than three decades of agitation, outrage, coercion and reconciliation before the land question was finally settled.

Parnell had two more years as 'a retiring country gentlemen of conservative tastes', as the anonymous compiler of *The Dictionary of National Biography* entry says he was regarded. Then in March 1874, three months before his twenty-eighth birthday, he called at Butt's home in Henrietta Street, Dublin, and offered himself to the cause of Home Rule. As Butt said, 'I have got a great recruit, young Parnell – a historic name – and unless I am mistaken, the Saxon will find him an ugly customer, though he is a damned good-looking fellow.' In fact he was to be the young king who would kill the old, but with his lack of forensic skills and unclubbable manner he did not seem then in any sense a rival. His first election campaign, in County Dublin, showed up his inadequacy as a public speaker and he was whipped at the polls. Yet on 22 April 1875 he took his seat as member for County Meath with the strong support of the local clergy and began the slow process of making himself an effective parliamentarian.

He soon realised that Butt's gentlemanly tactics were having little effect and that his limited definition of Home Rule – a kind of weak federalism with little clout except in local affairs – while having the virtue of not alarming conservatives at home and in Britain, was too limited to have wide support, especially after the Fenian activity. The effort, too, that the securing of his objectives would require against entrenched positions deserved a greater prize. Like Parnell, Butt would have liked to reconcile the Protestant Ascendancy to change and in so doing allow them to retain something of their political power. They could not see that accommodation to change was their only hope of survival and Butt their best means of achieving it. When, in October 1881, it was clear that Parnell would be arrested, he is supposed to have warned: 'Captain Moonlight [agrarian outrage] will take my place.' Butt could have threatened a much direr response to the landlords' failure to co-operate but he was too polite to utter it and they were too blind to respond. As it was, within four years the young recruit was the leader of the movement, in spite of having none of Butt's charm or skill in parliamentary speaking.

One of the most effective of Butt's lieutenants in the Irish Parliamentary Party was Joe Biggar (1828–90), an abrasive Belfast butcher who was MP for Cavan and had invented a device for the disruption of parliamentary business that he called 'obstructionism'. The technique included marathon speeches, often involving the slow recitation of pages of documents, newspaper reports and blue books that were already available in the library of the Commons and had been summarised in the House. Other delaying measures were amendments, the 'spying of strangers' – a delay of business while the serjeant-at-arms emptied the galleries (on one occasion the stranger 'spied' was the Prince of Wales) – and other entirely proper parliamentary procedures.

In Parnell's hands obstructionism became a

powerful means of making his presence felt and keeping Irish matters to the forefront. What was peculiarly galling to both Liberals and Conservatives – and embarrassing to Butt, who usually disliked the tactic – was that the Irish members did not confine their disruption to Irish business. On 27 July 1877 the House was kept in session between 4 and 6 pm the following day while the South Africa bill was being passed through committee. Probably the most outrageous example of obstructionism occurred in 1881, when Parnell led the Irish members in a filibuster to attempt to talk down the coercion measure known as the Protection of Persons and Property Bill, introduced by W. E. Forster (1819–86), the chief secretary, whom Parnell had effectively nicknamed 'Buckshot' Forster because he had given permission for the use of shot in quelling Irish riots. The bill was introduced by the unpopular Forster after a year of extremely serious agrarian unrest. The techniques of the 1870s were used again so that the House was in continuous session for forty-one-and-a-half hours from 4 pm on Monday 31 January until 9.30 pm on Wednesday 2 February. The Speaker was forced to modify existing procedures and introduce the right of 'closure', known commonly as the 'guillotine motion'. Although this spelt the end of extreme obstructionism, other tactics to disrupt the work of Parliament were quickly devised.

When Parnell first took his seat, the Irish members were little regarded, but by the time of Butt's retirement in 1879 Parnell had made the Irish Party a united, well-disciplined and politically significant force in British politics. They could find themselves holding the balance of power between the two major parties, and although he knew that he was likely to gain more from the Liberal Gladstone than from either Lord Salisbury (1830-1903) or even Benjamin Disraeli (1804–81), Parnell was perfectly willing for his purposes to make an alliance with the Tories. Individual MPs had considerably more independence and whips less power at that time than in twentieth-century politics. In fact Parnell's eventual alliance with the Liberals was not established until 1885, when Salisbury, leading a Tory government from the Lords, set his face firmly against Home Rule.

Parnell's austere mien and apparently unemotional behaviour always worried his opponents and perplexed his followers. They literally did not know what he was thinking or what he would do next. (This reputation was to help him when, in February 1886, he was forced for personal reasons to impose the extremely unsuitable Willie O'Shea as nationalist candidate upon the voters in the Galway by-election.) There were several constant elements in his character: his pragmatism (at times opportunism); his ability to maintain a party of followers with a wide ideological spectrum, from near-unionism to extreme republicanism; his self-confidence; his passion and flair for leadership; and his innate conservatism, which wished heartily to preserve his class and which led him ceaselessly to aim for détente between the southern Protestant ascendancy and the majority population. His fall and tragically early death meant that he did not succeed in his aims;

he had little support from his peers and his obtuseness in his attitude to Ulster must call into question the basis for his thrilling claim in Galway on the occasion of the foisting of O'Shea: 'I have a parliament for Ireland in the hollow of my hand.'

Just how strong the sense of betrayal was among Parnell's peers may be gauged from a comment, expressed with typical hunting metaphors, by Violet Martin (1862–1915), the 'Martin Ross' of the *Irish R.M.* stories, in her unfinished monograph 'The Martins of Ross', in *Irish Memories* (1917):

> With the close of the 'seventies came the burst into the open of the Irish Parliamentary Party, in full cry. Like hounds hunting confusedly in covert, they had, in the hands of Isaac Butt, kept up a certain amount of noise and excitement, keen, yet uncertain as to what game was on foot. From 1877 it was Parnell who carried the horn, a grim, disdainful Master, whose pack never dared to get closer to him than the length of his thong; but

he laid them on the line, and they ran it like wolves.

Martin, it must be said, was much more unionist in her politics than Edith Somerville (who was on good terms with Michael Collins), and her attitudes were undoubtedly coloured by the fact that a few generations before, the Martins of Ross had been Catholics.

Parnell was cheerful about his lack of rhetorical skills and bore stoically the terrible stress that public speaking imposed on him; because of his indomitable will he improved. One of his favourite locutions was: 'Speeches are not business!' What *was* business was the use he made of opportunities, especially at the beginning of his career, for making his presence felt – for 'bulging', to use the contemporary term. He walked a tightrope, using as balancing rod the width of his support. Perhaps a better metaphor might be that of the skill of the plate-spinner, a popular act in the music halls of his time. The artiste could keep up to twenty plates spinning on flexible canes while he moved casually about, reaching a faltering plate just as it seemed about to topple.

In 1875 he engaged in a public and – it seemed to many more besides Butt – undignified squabble about the funds for the celebration of the centenary of Daniel O'Connell's birth; in 1876 he objected in the House to the Manchester martyrs being called murderers and caused a furore nationwide; in a further show of solidarity with the Fenians he joined the Amnesty Association and urged that they be treated as political prisoners; he won the confidence – or at least the collaboration – of John Devoy (1842–1928), the permanent Fenian exile and chief of Clan na Gael, who continued to have a strong influence on Irish politics, both constitutional and otherwise, until the founding of the Irish Free State; he repeatedly brought up the case of his coeval Michael Davitt (1846–1906), the one-armed IRB member from Straide, near Foxford, County Mayo, who was a prisoner in Dartmoor because of arms smuggling and was eventually released on ticket-of-leave in December 1877 (he was one of the party that welcomed him home to Dublin); he refused to condemn the murderers of the notorious Lord Leitrim in

1878 and he made William O'Brien (1852–
1928) and John Dillon (1851–1927), the
agrarian militants, his closest lieutenants –
though considering the nature of the Chief
that was not very close.

The recurring question of landlordism
and tenant proprietorship was to give him
the greatest power and make him the 'uncrowned king' of Ireland, though in lending
his weight to the ultimate success of the
Land War he effectively brought about the
destruction of the very class he tried to
save. He hoped that with the successful
achievement of limited agrarian reforms he
might use his power and his 'army' to
concentrate on the ultimate goal of a Dublin
parliament which would ensure that Irishmen
(including the 'natural' ascendancy leaders of his
own class) should settle their own affairs. The
New Departure, as the agreement made in 1879
between Devoy, Davitt and Parnell was known,
meant that the IRB and Clan na Gael would
pursue a policy that was constitutional in that
it generally stopped short of actual violence.
Initially Parnell had had to be persuaded to

support the agitation because he was reluctant to offend the Church and the increasing number of Catholics who had substantial holdings. He was not really in favour of Davitt's ideal, inherited from John Fintan Lalor (1807–49), of peasant proprietorship; it was too socialistic and the agitation that its achievement would require would distract from his main objective – separation from Britain. Being an essentially practical politician, however, he saw that such concentration of energies would give him greater control over the peacetime Fenians and allow him to make sure that agrarian agitation should become not an end in itself but another advance towards the goal of independence.

3

THE LAND WAR

The poor weather and bad harvests in the concluding years of the 1870s again brought the spectre of famine and its customary grisly companion, eviction. It also provided Devoy and Davitt with fertile conditions for a new kind of Fenian activity. When they met Parnell in 1878 not long after the latter's release they laid before him the principles of their New Departure, a plan of campaign that had not been approved by the IRB: self-government rather than a loose federalism was to be their stated aim; the ultimate goal of any land agitation (or 'war', as it was more accurately termed later) was to be 'on the basis of peasant proprietary'; sectarian issues were to excluded; the Irish Party were to be whipped in and were to pursue an aggressive policy that would include resistance to any coercive measures; and (with more piety than practicality) they were 'to advocate the cause of all struggling nationalities in the British Empire and elsewhere'.

Parnell was slow to respond; for one thing he was not an advocate of tenant ownership, preferring to forge a working alliance between the existing landlords (many of them by now Catholics) and amenable tenants. He always needed to avoid alienating the Catholic Church, which was bound by canon law to be constitutionalist unless under extreme circumstances, and though he could always count on the support of his constituency clergy he was regarded by many clerics with nearly as much suspicion as the IRB and Clan na Gael. A week before the important public meeting at Westport, County Mayo, on 8 June 1879, John MacHale (1791–1881), Archbishop of Tuam, O'Connell's old ally, wrote a letter to the *Freeman's Journal* warning against attendance. (MacHale was then nearly ninety and it was generally believed that it was his Cullenite secretary who was the actual correspondent.)

Parnell's reluctance was finally overcome by

the man among his followers who was closest to him in attitudes. This was Andrew J. Kettle, the father of Thomas Kettle, who became a leading constitutional nationalist MP and was killed at Guinchy on the Somme. Kettle had founded the County Dublin Tenants Defence Association but would participate in no activity that was outside the law. He would settle for the 'three "F"s' (fair rent, fixity of tenure, free sale) as an intermediate measure. The Irish National Land League was founded on 21 October 1879 at a meeting at which Kettle was in the chair and Parnell was made its president. The organisation's stated aims were to secure the reduction of rack rents and 'to facilitate the obtaining of the ownership of the soil by the occupiers'. It was a formula sufficiently vague to satisfy all the parties involved.

Mayo, still shaken by the famine of twenty-five years before, now faced the threat of a repetition of the horror and was therefore the appropriate place to start the agitation. The Westport meeting, with 4,000 attending in spite of heavy rain and the Archbishop's interdict, was held on 8 June 1879, and though one speaker declared that Home Rule agitation was useless in a parliament filled with landlords, Parnell remained impassive. His own speech was fiery enough to please even the physical-force people: 'You must show the landlords that you intend to keep a firm grip of your homesteads. You must not allow yourself to be dispossessed as you were dispossessed in 1847.' Even more memorable was his speech advocating social ostracism, delivered at Ennis on Sunday 19 September 1880. Asked what should be done with 'a tenant who bids for a farm from which his neighbour has been evicted', he said, beginning with a feline purr:

> Now I think I heard somebody say, 'Shoot him!' but I wish to point out to you a much better way – a more Christian, a more charitable way – which will give the lost sinner an opportunity of repenting. When a man takes a farm from which another has been evicted, you must show him on the roadside when you meet him, you must show him in the streets of the town, you must show him at the shop

counter, you must show him in the fair and at the market place and even in the house of worship, by leaving him severely alone, by putting him into a sort of moral Coventry, by isolating him from the rest of his kind as if he were a leper of old, you must show him your detestation of the crime he has committed.

It proved a very effective and cruel weapon; even as he spoke, its most famous application was in operation at the home near Lough Mask in County Mayo of Captain Charles Cunningham Boycott (1832–97), himself a small landlord but unpopular as the agent in the county for Lord Erne. He was unable to save his harvest since none of the local labourers would work for him. Eventually he imported 150 Orangemen from Cavan but they required 7,000 soldiers and police to protect them from reprisal. It was an expensive way of bringing in the harvest, and Boycott, unable even to find a hotel in Dublin, temporarily withdrew from the country altogether. The event also gave the language a very useful word. Boycotting was clearly effective but it lent itself too easily to local abuse; personal vendettas and old antagonisms were as often the basis for its infliction as the breaking of the league's rules. The heightened level of violent activity meant that the youth of the country went their adrenalin-driven way, and burning of hayricks and 'houghing' of cattle were done much in the spirit of the old secret societies and of sheer anarchy. Captain Moonlight was riding again.

In fact 'emergency men' organised by the Orange Order could usually be found to 'volunteer' to help break boycotts but they were rarely required in Ulster and were not asked to penetrate too deeply into nationalist territory. The Land League had quickly garnered members in Catholic Ulster, where conditions of rental were slanted more in favour of the tenants – the famous 'Ulster custom'. Davitt tried to woo Protestants, using a different rhetoric to suit the 'hard, cold fire of the Northerner'. They had been engaged in a struggle with their own landlords and were glad of the countrywide agitation. The Loyal Order, however, was soon able to persuade the majority that the Land League was a nationalist organisation, using its own terse vocabulary of vituperation. As it turned out, the Ulster tenants achieved all they required with Gladstone's Land Law (Ireland) Act of 1881.

Distracted by events nearer home, Davitt – and, with less excuse, Parnell – lost an opportunity to engage with these other Irishmen, who were to continue to resist anything with a 'nationalist' tag. They were as strongly against Home Rule as the House of Lords and felt that they had much more to lose from it. They would never, as one of their comic ballads would put it, 'forsake the oul' cause/That gave us our freedom, religion and laws.' Home Rule meant, even then, 'Rome Rule', and that raucous parrot cry has been heard ever since. One of the great 'ifs' of Irish history is the consideration of what might have happened if Parnell had engaged the northern Protestants with the same concentration as in other aspects of his policy. Perhaps here his Katharine-based distraction was most lethal; he believed that the few nights' rioting in the Shankill and

Ballymacarret that would be the only serious response to a Home Rule bill would be easily contained by the RIC and that the Ulster Protestants would soon see sense in a way for which they were supposed to be famous.

He was no historian, unlike his northern adversaries, who could give graphic details of 1641 and celebrate Derry, Aughrim, Enniskillen and the Boyne. He must have been aware that the Tories, determined to do down Gladstone and preserve the integrity of the ever-growing empire, would use every trick they could devise. It was the brilliant and ruthless Lord Randolph Churchill (1849–94) who spoke the words that others were thinking when in 1866 he wrote, 'I decided some time ago that if the GOM ['grand old man' – Gladstone] went for Home Rule the Orange card would be the one to play.' He later reassured a huge crowd of supporters in the Ulster Hall in Belfast on 26 February 1886: 'Ulster at the proper moment will resort to the supreme arbitrament of force. Ulster will fight and Ulster will be right.' He managed, too, to give the impression that a Conservative government would not betray them to Rome Rule. (He had lived in Dublin from 1877 until 1880 as secretary to his father, the Lord Lieutenant, and had got to know the politics of the place well. He noted presciently, 'Personal jealousies, government influences, Davitt, Fenian intrigue will all be at work, and the bishops, who in their heart of hearts hate Parnell and don't care a scrap for Home Rule, will complete the rout.')

The minor crisis had thrown up the usual effective demagogues: William Johnston (1829–1902) 'of Ballykilbeg' and Colonel Edward James Saunderson (1837–1906) were the Carson and Craig of their day and their agitation was a kind of dress rehearsal for 1913, with the same kind of threats of armed resistance, expressed with biblical imagery and the conviction that the Tories would supply the arms if they were needed. As it was, the Lords ditched the bill and the crisis passed but it was clear that Parnell's response was not sufficiently focused. If he had been able to lead his party during the 1890s he might have come to some kind of working arrangement with the northern unionists. Their leaders lacked the appeal of later paladins, and

Gladstone was a man of much greater power, integrity and courage than Asquith. Fate and history decided otherwise.

During the last months of 1879, while the Land War continued, Parnell and Dillon toured America, to rapturous acclaim. The son of 'Old Ironsides' was acceptable to the Yankee grandees as well as to the Tammany Irish, and the dollars rolled in. A sum of £70,000 (more than £2,000,000 in today's money) was spent largely on charitable relief of the near-famine in the vulnerable areas. When Parnell hastened home on hearing that a general election had been called for April 1880, he came as, in the words of his adversarial colleague Tim Healy (1855–1931), 'the uncrowned king of Ireland'. He was elected for Cork, Mayo and Meath, as the plural system of the time permitted. Sixty-seven Home Rulers, of whom twenty-seven were Parnellites, had been elected, but significantly Gladstone was returned with a majority – and the ever-firmer determination to find the answer to the Irish question.

The news from Ireland, especially in the west and south, continued to be bad. Rents were withheld and evictions resisted. The number of agrarian crimes rose from 301 in 1878, to 869 in 1879, to 2,590 in 1880 and to 4,431 in 1881. Parnell, Healy and other members of the league were prosecuted for the general lawlessness that they apparently fostered. The jury failed to agree on a verdict and it was clear that any fairly empanelled jury would never find the Chief guilty. Chief Secretary Forster's response was the bill, which, as we have seen, was the occasion of the last stand of 'obstructionism', with the marathon sitting of February 1881. It granted the power to magistrates in designated areas to suspend habeas corpus, especially in matters dealing with the possession and acquisition of arms, and since the ordinary judicial process could not achieve the purpose of imprisoning Parnell and his activists, arrangements for internment without trial were put in train. Davitt's ticket-of-leave was rescinded on 2 February and it was known that it was only a matter of time before the rest of the league's leaders would join him in prison.

With a slightly clumsy compensatory gesture, Gladstone introduced his land bill on 7 April, and by 16 August it had passed the Lords. (The coercion bill had had to come first to reassure the upper house.) It granted the three 'F's with an official land court to fix fair rents, which would remain unchanged for fifteen years. The court in time became the Land Commission, which would finally settle the quest of land ownership – although not precisely as either Parnell or Davitt wished. If such an act had been passed in any of the previous three decades, it would have been received with jubilation, but now agitation had become a habit and about 20 per cent of farmers who had serious arrears were not permitted to approach the commission until their debts were paid. Parnell was publicly unimpressed, though he stated privately that the bill's provisions were all he required from the agitation. Yet he made no move to call off the 'war'; he was anxious to seem to be as resolutely anti-British as the IRB or Clan na Gael. He needed their support for the next and greater prize – an independent parliament which would in time become completely separate from Britain.

In fact the arrest of Parnell and his chief lieutenants on 13 October was a relief and an

unwitting gift from Gladstone. The austere
Chief was relieved of decision-making at a time
when his private life was beginning to impinge
upon his public affairs, and he was able to
taste the fate and share the glory of all true-
born Irishmen. His seven months in Kilmainham were no more penal than O'Connell's in Richmond thirty-seven years earlier.
The Kilmainham 'committee', which was
conveniently located in the same building, issued
a 'no-rent' manifesto on 18 October, and, as if
on cue, Forster suppressed the Land League two
days later. Parnell was no doubt pleased. Captain
Moonlight obliged with spasmodic affrays, and
Parnell's sisters – Fanny (1849–82) in America
and Anna (1852–1911) in Ireland – carried on
the work of the suppressed organisation. Anna
was vigorous in her duties, holding meetings,
resisting evictions and organising accommodation for the evicted and drawing freely on the
league's substantial funds. When Parnell was
eventually released, he suppressed her organisation (which was known, with typical Victorian
genteelness, as the Ladies' Land League) by
stopping access to the funds, and he and his

sister became estranged. Fanny had died in 1882 while trying to organise the same kind of distaff group in the eastern United States.

For some time Forster persisted in his boast that his coercion act and internment of the troublemakers had been successful, but the outrages continued. Parliament was heartily sick of Irish affairs and negotiations were already under way to end the war between Parnell and Gladstone. The intermediaries on Parnell's side were Captain Willie O'Shea and his beautiful wife, Katharine, known to her friends as Katie and to her lover Parnell as Queenie. They met Joseph Chamberlain (1836–1914), who was the GOM's ablest lieutenant and who, though too much of an imperialist to contemplate Home Rule, wished Ireland to have strong local autonomy in a federalist union with Britain. Together they devised the terms of Parnell's release and the conditions for a true alliance with the Liberal Party; the resulting document became known as the 'Kilmainham Treaty'.

4

THE KILMAINHAM TREATY

On 2 May 1882 Parnell and his supporters walked free from Kilmainham to hear that Forster, feeling betrayed by Gladstone, had resigned and that the popular Lord Frederick Cavendish (1836–82) had been made Chief Secretary. The 'treaty' was essentially an agreement that, in return for the release of the internees and the acceptance by the land agitators of the terms of the 1881 act – with a satisfactory solution of the rent-arrears question – Parnell would make sure that rural unrest was quietened. The extra concession by Parnell of an alliance with the Liberals, which so delighted Gladstone ('a hors d'oeuvre which we had no right to expect'), was not intended as part of the deal. It suited Parnell well enough but was against his instinctive policy of non-alignment. Gladstone was right to feel 'indebted to O'Shea', who was the author of the agreement. O'Shea had felt himself in a strong enough position vis-à-vis Parnell to demand from him the authority to offer it in his negotiations with Chamberlain. It was to be the beginning of much grief from the same source; what was galling to the Chief was that the vain – and wayward – husband of his mistress was motivated not by political vision or concern for Ireland but simply by the wish to impress his patron, Chamberlain.

Davitt was released from Portland Prison in Dorset on 6 May and Parnell was there to meet him and convey him to London. The same day news came of the savage murder in Phoenix Park of Cavendish and the under-secretary, Thomas Burke (1829–82), by a group of extreme Fenians known as the Invincibles, who were armed with surgical knives. The detested Forster had been threatened many times, and Burke, who was a Castle Catholic and had once been Sir Robert Peel's private secretary, was probably the main target of the attack. As always, such groups flourished in a climate in which extreme coercive measures, including the setting up of the Special Irish Branch in Scotland Yard (the forerunner of the present-day anti-terrorist force), were implemented to combat terrorism. The government's reaction to the attack gave the Invincibles a short-term fame and allowed them to escape for a time the moral consequences of their actions. Parnell was horrified and offered to apply for the Chiltern Hundreds but his followers and Gladstone persuaded him to stay and do what he could to save the situation. The upsurge in terrorism left those in Britain who had been sympathetic to the Irish cause high and dry, and over the next three years a series of dynamite outrages (including attacks on the Houses of Parliament and the Tower of London) by a breakaway group of Clan na Gael Americans made things worse.

By now Parnell was a man torn between his public career and his deep love for Katharine. At times he felt, like Antony with Cleopatra, that the world was well lost, and it was only his amazing arrogance that persuaded him that he could effectively manage both sides of his life. Yet for a long time he succeeded in this aim. The quiet years (1882–5) witnessed the consolidation of his power. In 1883 it became known that he was in financial difficulties, owing £18,000, with Avondale heavily mortgaged. Parnell was an indulgent landlord and had spent a great deal of money besides on unprofitable mining schemes in Wicklow. A cheque for £37,000 (about £750,000 in today's terms) was given to him as a testimonial. Among the subscribers were Irish Church leaders, including Bishop Thomas Nulty (d. 1898) of Meath and the more famous Archbishop Thomas Croke of Cashel (1824–1902), who defied *De Parnellio,* a condemnatory circular from the Vatican – which was always susceptible to British diplomacy – to take part in the scheme. Parnell continued to avail himself of the services of priests at the constituency level, and when William J. Walsh (1841–1921) became Archbishop of Dublin he found an ally who wanted to take an active part in the selection of candidates.

In 1884 the egregious O'Shea had assumed the powers of a plenipotentiary and was engaged with Chamberlain in a thorough reform of Irish local government which proposed the setting up of a central board which should have limited legislative powers. This was Chamberlain's idea for killing the demands for Home Rule. Parnell's response was a famous speech, part of which was inscribed on the plinth of his memorial statue, which stands between O'Connell Street and Parnell Square. It was given in his Cork constituency on 21 January 1885:

> No man has a right to say to his country: 'Thus far shalt you go and no further,' and we have never attempted to fix the *ne plus ultra* to the progress of Ireland's nationhood, and we never shall.

This speech was his most famous but it was also in a way his emptiest since it is not clear just what he meant by it and it is certain that the fact that it provided material for later rhetoric would have embarrassed him. These later interpretations took his words far beyond his own ambitions for Ireland.

The Liberals were not only split over the Chamberlain proposals but were also set to impose further coercive measures. When the government fell, in June, it was defeated by a temporary alliance between the Conservatives and the Irish Party, and the Chief looked for some tangible evidence of promises at which Churchill had hinted. One useful result of the brief flirtation was Lord Ashbourne's Purchase of Land Act, which permitted 100 per cent loans to tenants who wished to buy their properties. In the general election of November of that year the Irish were urged by Parnell to turn against the Liberals. The vote had been granted to most heads of households by the 1884 Franchise Act, and while the Liberals obtained eighty-six more seats than the Tories, this was exactly the number of nationalist MPs that Parnell controlled – eighty-five in Ireland and T. P. O'Connor (1848–1929), who represented Liverpool (Scotland) and continued to do so until his death in 1929. Parnell was near the zenith of his power and it was clear that, with the land troubles at least on the way to being solved, the Irish Party was now intent on achieving Home Rule. (William O'Brien's 'Plan of Campaign', not supported by Parnell, continued to little effect until 1891, when the Balfour Act confirmed the impression that the achievement of tenant ownership was merely a matter of time.)

The party's commitment to Home Rule was sharpened by the flying in December of the 'Hawarden Kite' by Herbert Gladstone (1854–1930), the GOM's youngest son. (The Gladstone family seat was Hawarden Castle in present-day Clwyd.) This 'indiscreet' statement that his father was about to declare for Home Rule was repudiated by Gladstone but from then on it was clear that he had decided that it was the next – and perhaps the last – element of Irish 'pacification' and that the Conservatives had set their faces against it. On 8 April 1886 Gladstone introduced a bill for the establishment of an Irish parliament with wide domestic powers but excluding control of armed forces, coinage and customs and excise. This was not a very revolutionary proposal and it included a contribution to the imperial exchequer of £3,244,000, a tribute which Parnell called 'a hard bargain'. It was too much, however, for the Chamberlain radicals, who helped defeat it at the second reading, and it caused serious rioting in an easily inflamed Belfast. Parnell showed less-than-full understanding of the nature of the problem, stating in a speech in Plymouth on 26 June that '1,000 men of the Royal Irish Constabulary will be amply sufficient to cope with all the rowdies that the Orangemen can produce.' Perhaps if the government had been strong and united and the Conservatives, led by Churchill, less irresponsible in their tactics, 1,000 RIC men and 1,000 soldiers might have settled the matter once and for all.

In the election that followed the defeat of the bill, Salisbury's party was returned with a majority which enabled it to dominate politics until 1906, though Gladstone introduced another unsuccessful bill in his last short administration (1892–4). For the next few years Parnell effectively ceased to have a political life – he rarely attended Parliament and made few public appearances. He lived in Katharine's house in the south-eastern London suburb of Eltham, which was then a village on the road to Chatham, in, as the contemporary satirist W. S. Gilbert put it, 'the felicity of unbounded domesticity'. These quiet years were interrupted in 1887 by the Piggott affair. Between March and December 1887 the *Times* published a series of articles, entitled 'Parnellism and Crime', in which the suspicions of part of the English electorate were confirmed. The articles suggested that Parnell, as indicated in a series of letters by him, was involved in terrorism. One in particular, dated 15 May 1882 and published on 18 April, said that 'though I regret the accident of Lord F. Cavendish's death I cannot refuse to admit that Burke got more than his deserts.'

Parnell denounced the letter as 'a villainous and bare-faced forgery' but took no further action in the matter. The style of the letters was clearly not his and he was prepared to let the matter go, with his usual disdain. He also suspected that it was his nemesis, O'Shea, who had made the forgeries. Frank Hugh O'Donnell, a former and irascible colleague of Parnell's who had been mentioned in the forged letters, brought an action for libel on his own behalf. The *Times* responded with another letter on 18 April; it was dated 9 January 1882 and contained the words: 'This inaction is inexcusable . . . Let there be an end to this hesitancy. Prompt action is called for. You undertook to make it hot for Forster and Co.' The Salisbury government, which was as anxious as the *Times* to incriminate Parnell, established a special commission to investigate the business. The bill authorising the commission became law on 11 August 1888 and on the same day Parnell sued the newspaper for libel, claiming damages of £100,000. All the leaders of the Land League were arraigned as respondents as part of a grand conspiracy against 'the English garrison'. The government paraded many witnesses who gave testimony about agrarian agitation and actual crimes, and it was clear that in the circumstances the commission would find against the whole movement.

On 21 February Richard Piggott (c. 1828–89), a nationalist journalist and editor, was called as a witness. He had once owned three periodicals, the *Irishman*, the *Shamrock* and the *Flag of Ireland,* but he lived such a rackety life that he had had to sell them to the Land League in 1881. Since then he had made what living he could by writing anonymous, libellous pamphlets

about his former associates. He had supplied
information about Parnell and the others leaders
of the league to Edward Caulfield Houston, the
secretary of the Irish Loyal and Patriotic
Union, the leading anti-Home Rule society,
who had passed them on to the *Times*. His
evidence included the forged letters, for
which Houston had paid him £605. His
evidence collapsed under the relentless
cross-questioning of Parnell's counsel, Sir
Charles Russell (1832–1900), who afterwards, as Lord Russell of Killowen, became
the first Catholic Lord Chief Justice since the
Reformation. At the end of that day's hearing
Piggott fled to Spain and a week later he
committed suicide in a Madrid hotel.

At once the tension went out of the situation;
the commission continued to sit and the members
of the Irish Party gave somewhat dusty answers.
The Liberals were perfectly satisfied with the
demolition of Piggott's evidence and, regarding
it as a complete acquittal, publicly congratulated
Parnell. In December Gladstone invited Parnell
to Hawarden, where the two men discussed –
without much agreement but with much greater

Vanity Fair cartoon of Charles Stewart Parnell
(Mansell Collection/Time Inc/Katz Pictures)

Parnell's home in Avondale, Rathdrum, County Wicklow
(Hulton Getty Picture Collection)

Land League meeting at Kildare on 3 January 1881: Michael
J. Boyton burns the Duke of Leinster's leases on a "98 pike"
(Illustrated London News Picture Library)

British Prime Minister Gladstone, under the influence of the
Land League, signing the revolutionary Land Bill of 1881
(National Library of Ireland)

Gladstone speaking in favour of the Home Rule Bill in the
House of Commons on 8 April 1886
(Illustrated London News Picture Library)

amity and mutual respect than they had had for each other before – the details of future Home Rule proposals. (Apart from remarkable courage and determination, the two shared an almost total lack of humour. Parnell once at an election meeting introduced A. J. Kettle with the words, 'And now a man whose name is a household word', and looked bewildered when everyone laughed.) The commission's report was published on 13 February 1890; it exonerated Parnell of any complicity in a crime but censured him for his failure to denounce the perpetrators openly. Gladstone asked the House to express 'its reprobation of the false charges of the gravest and most odious description based upon calumny and forgery' and described Parnell as the victim 'of a frightful outrage' to whom reparation was due 'in the name of Christian charity'.

The stage was set for the presentation in the next parliament of a Home Rule bill which would pass the Commons on a strong Liberal–Parnellite alliance. There was time to work out a formula which would satisfy the broad centre of nationalists while not frightening the English Liberals. Parnell, though ill and weak, was at the height of his popularity and power but the wild card O'Shea had already filed a petition for divorce on the ground of his wife's adultery, naming Parnell as co-respondent. In Aristotelian terms Parnell was about to be destroyed by his nemesis and, at a more vulgar level, the curtain was rising on the last act of the melodrama.

5

UNCROWNED QUEEN

The Englishwoman whom Parnell met for the first time on 30 July 1880 and with whom he fell almost immediately in love was born Katharine Wood on 31 January 1845, the youngest child of the Rev Sir Page Wood. The family were upper-middle-class Whigs and an uncle had been Lord Chancellor in Gladstone's first administration. She was darkly beautiful and, though without formal education, quick and intelligent. She was known as Katie to her family and husband, Queenie or Wifie to her lover and Kitty only to Tim Healy and the press. (At that time the word had a strong sexual connotation and was never used in a friendly way.) Being sophisticated and interested in literature and politics, she was on friendly terms with the novelists Anthony Trollope and George

Meredith and was used to entertaining many liberal statesmen at her father's table.

Her husband-to-be was Irish, Catholic and, like herself, a member of a prosperous family. Born in Dublin in 1840, the son of a wealthy solicitor, William Henry O'Shea (pronounced to rhyme with 'bee') behaved throughout his sixty-five years like a character from a William Thackeray or Charles Lever novel. He was handsome, vain, feckless, ambitious, spendthrift, socially charming and rather stupid. His father, who patiently paid his son's huge debts at Oscott and during his short stay at Trinity, purchased a commission in the fashionable Eighteenth Hussars for him. He continued to foot the bill for William's extravagances until his death in 1866. Katharine married O'Shea on 24 January 1867 with no apparent enthusiasm and the couple went to live in Spain. Willie's uncle John was a banker in Madrid, and as a sign of maturity – spurious, as it turned out – he sold his commission for £4,000 and invested the proceeds in a partnership.

He soon quarrelled with John, returned to England and bankrupted himself attempting to

run a stud farm in Hertfordshire. By the time
he had failed as the manager of a sulphur mine,
again in Spain, he had ceased to cohabit with
Katharine, spending most of his time in London.
She was maintained by her wealthy widowed
aunt, Mrs Benjamin Wood, and a substantial
amount of the money Katharine received in this
way ended up in Willie's pocket. In 1875 she
became Aunt Ben's companion, living in a villa
supplied by her at Eltham, close to her own
house. Though Willie led his own life in
London, gambling and indulging in casual
liaisons, he still visited Katharine from time
to time. By now they had three children –
a boy and two girls – who were a con-
siderable consolation to her in what was a
lonely and inevitably dull life. Like many
other women of her time, class and talents,
she felt that there should be more to existence than maternity and the supervision of
housekeeping.

By the time Parnell was arrested Katharine
was pregnant with their first child, and while on
compassionate licence from Kilmainham to
attend the funeral of his nephew in Paris he was

able to visit Eltham and hold his dying daughter, Claude Sophie, in his arms. Katharine had had a kind of nervous breakdown during the pregnancy; this breakdown had been brought on by the strain of the fact that she and her husband lived apart. They had communicated as well as they could, often with messages in invisible ink, and the baby had at first been quite healthy. The child died while Parnell and Willie were at Eltham working on the details of the Kilmainham Treaty. Two more daughters were to be born to them: Clare on 4 March 1883 and Katie on 27 November 1884.

Much has been said and written on how complaisant O'Shea may have been with regard to the relationship. His temperament was such that he could maintain a high tolerance of the condition psychologists call denial. He may have believed that Claude Sophie was his child since sexual relations between him and Katharine continued after her meeting with Parnell. It was to his advantage to remain in some association with her since her dole from Aunt Ben supported him. It also supported Parnell. One of the reasons for O'Shea's filing for divorce was his discovery that he had been specifically excluded from the enjoyment of the substantial legacy that was to come to Katharine. From 1880 he tried politics as a last career, representing Clare from 1880 to 1885 as a member of the Irish Party, though he was far from an ideal represent-ative: he rejected party discipline, refused to vote or even sit with other members and was lax in constituency business. His defeat as a Liberal in a Liverpool constituency in the 1885 election came as no surprise to anyone but himself, and it was then that Parnell took the great risk of forcing him upon the reluctant voters of Galway in 1886.

His refusal to support the Home Rule bill was perfectly logical since he was a unionist and had never felt any affinity with the Parnellites. He applied for the Chiltern Hundreds the day after the division and for a time passed out of both Katharine's life and the public eye. Aunt Ben died, aged ninety-six, on 19 May 1899, leaving her fortune of £140,000 entirely to Katharine. Immediately, her brothers and sisters, who had earlier tried to have Aunt Ben found incompetent, began to contest the will, and so not only would O'Shea get none of her money but also, because the will remained in probate for three years, there was none available for Katharine to buy him off. If the £20,000 that O'Shea would have accepted to go away and not rock the boat had been available, the disastrous divorce case might not have taken place.

As it was, Parnell's response was characteristically inert. He would not let Katharine enter a counter-plea, though she was anxious to wound Willie. There are several possible explanations for Parnell's lack of response. He was physically at a low ebb, looking much older than his forty-three years, and was disinclined to ruffle the comfort of his rather staid domestic existence with Katharine in Brighton, where they had moved after Aunt Ben's death. At times he may have felt that this cosier private life was worth the ending of his political career. Again he wanted to marry Katharine, and her divorce from the pestilent Willie was the only way to achieve this. Moreover, considering the nature of his temperament and his doughty dismissal of the *Times* campaign, he may have felt that his

Olympian good luck would somehow hold; inaction during crises in the past had proved the best means of dealing with them.

Although it lasted only two days, the case was sensational: the press at the time spared no item of evidence that was presented. Since no defence was entered, all the public heard were the sordid and ludicrous details of the affair presented by Sir Edward Clarke, Willie's counsel. A decree nisi with costs against Parnell was granted on 17 November, and he and Katharine were married in a registry office at Steyning, near Brighton, on 25 June 1891. They had hoped for a church service but none of the local Anglican clergy would perform the ceremony. The time of the ceremony – 8.30 in the morning – was chosen to avoid the attentions of the press, Parnell having told his groom to have the carriage ready at eleven, expecting, correctly, that he would leak the story.

After the divorce, Gladstone and the Irish Party held their breath, and the Irish Church, contrary to popular belief, was silent. On 25 November, Parnell was unanimously elected chairman of his party, and many hoped this would be the occasion of a discreet and dignified resignation. How wrong they were became clear when three days later he issued a swingeing attack on the Liberal party and revealed details of the confidential discussions he had had with Gladstone the previous December at Hawarden. It was clear that he was, in the words of Hugh Gaitskell (1902–63), a politician whose career was also terminated by an untimely death, going 'to fight, fight and fight again'. By then, Gladstone, who had been prepared to allow him to keep his position, had learned from the nonconformist wing of his party that they would no longer support Home Rule with Parnell as leader of the Irish Party. Gladstone was left with no option and his open letter to his Chief Secretary, John Morley (1838–1923), made it clear that 'notwithstanding the splendid services rendered by Mr Parnell to his country, his continuance at the present moment in the leadership would be productive of consequences disastrous in the highest degree to the cause of Ireland.'

Cecil Rhodes (1853–1902), the empire-builder who had sent Parnell £10,000 for Home

Rule funds in July 1888 on condition that he agree to the retention of the Irish members in the House even if an Irish parliament were obtained, sent a succinct cable from Cape Colony: 'Resign – marry – return.' It was sensible advice but unlikely to move the gaunt, ill but suddenly dynamic Chief. As Katharine recalled in her memoir, when, early in their relationship, she had chided him for treating his party members with scant courtesy, he replied, 'You must learn the ethics of kingship, Queenie: never explain, never apologise . . . I could never keep my rabble together if I were not above the human weakness of apology.' The remark was conversational and private but seems appropriate to his character.

He was to face his 'rabble' in Committee Room 15 in the House on 1 December 1890 and by now the battle lines between the faithful and the anti-Parnellites had already been drawn up. The party had known about Katharine since the time of the Galway by-election. The crack 'O'Shea Who Must Be Obeyed' – a pun on the main character in the popular romance of the day, *She* (1887), by H. Rider Haggard (1856–

1925) – was an old one by the time it was used as a caption for one of *Vanity Fair*'s famous cartoons. Now old animosities were stirring and resentment at cavalier treatment was leading to a dramatic confrontation which was to leave Parnell as the chief of only a third of his party members. In spite of personal feelings, however, the main concern of all the parties was the Home Rule cause. After the Chief's fall and death the agitation was to continue, led by less charismatic leaders, and when the chance came to push the legislation through both Houses there was no British statesman who possessed either the calibre or the genuine commitment to Ireland of Gladstone.

6

COMMITTEE ROOM 15

Parnell arranged that Room 15 in the House of Commons be used for the meeting of the party, which had been requisitioned by a majority of members. Already old associates such as Dillon, O'Connor and O'Brien had called for a change of leadership, and Archbishops Walsh and Croke added their support to the anti-Parnell lobby. The Church representatives had held off until then, conscious of how effective any denunciation by them would be and how potentially damaging to the cause the ensuing rancour would prove. In the prevailing moral climate, the clergy could not be seen to continue to support a public adulterer who was about to be disowned by his own colleagues. They could not appear to be less righteous than Gladstone's chapel members.

At first Parnell tried to have any discussion

of his future ruled out of order but a friendly motion to postpone the main business was lost by forty-four votes to twenty-nine. He then tried to focus on Gladstone's possible initiatives, offering to resign if the GOM could promise a significant Home Rule measure, but no such undertaking was given. The level of debate, which had until then been serious and high-minded, began to deteriorate as the members grew impatient with Parnell's adamant refusal to listen to them. One of his supporters, John Redmond (1856–1918), who afterwards brought a united party closer to Home Rule achieved by constitutional means than anyone else, referred to Gladstone as 'the master of the party', and Tim Healy, already known as Parnell's chief critic and feared for his savage wit, responded with, 'Who is to be mistress of the party?' Parnell rose to strike him and from that moment it was clear that there was no hope of avoiding a serious schism.

Healy, who was probably the first to make the 'she-who-must-be-obeyed' jibe, was to lead the anti-Parnell campaign over the next, crucial nine months and resort to much more bitter and vituperative language, but he never quite achieved the position he might have hoped to attain. Though he was to be the first Governor-General of the Irish Free State, his political career effectively died with Parnell. It was Justin McCarthy (1830–1912) – who managed to stay on friendly terms with Parnell afterwards – who led forty-five members out of the room and left the Chief with just twenty-seven loyal supporters. By now Archbishop Walsh's formal call to Irish Catholics to repudiate him had been published, and though some of the clergy refused to join in the condemnation a majority made their anti-Parnellite views known from many pulpits. As Robert Kee records in *The Green Flag* (1972), one Wicklow parish priest announced to his startled flock, 'Parnellism is a simple love of adultery, and all those who profess Parnellism profess to love and admire adultery', and warned them against letting Parnellites into their houses 'for they will do all they can to commit these adulteries'.

This was a case of extreme enthusiasm but the country as a whole followed the clergy's instructions, as they had been accustomed to doing for forty years. Parnell still retained a great following in Dublin and Cork. When he arrived at Kingstown he was cheered, and Healy, who had travelled on the same steamer, was hissed. It had been some time since Parnell had been home, and his intensity was palpable. The inertia was gone, replaced by a terrible energy. He was plainly ill, with eyes terrible to look at – except when he appeared with a bandage over the right one after an attack on 16 December at Castlecomer during the by-election campaign for Vincent Scully in north Kilkenny. One of the miners had thrown a white powder in his eyes: the Parnellites (and James Joyce) said it was quicklime; the Healyites claimed it was flour. Even then, with his tall, almost emaciated figure and blanched cheeks, except where hectic spots burned, he looked like an avenging angel or an Old Testament prophet.

One unlikely episode in the last campaign that he afterwards recounted with schoolboy glee was his storming of the offices of *United Ireland* – the paper he had founded and whose editor, Matthew Bodkin, he had dismissed as an anti-Parnellite. After his hugely successful meeting at the Rotunda on 10 December, the offices were taken over by a group of opponents. Parnell, like any modern action hero, rushed to the building, on O'Connell Street, pushed his way through the crowd of his supporters, seized a crowbar and smashed in the main door. The occupants left discreetly by the back door.

It was one of his few successes: in spite of vigorous campaigning in by-elections in North Kilkenny in December, North Sligo in March and Carlow in July, all his candidates were beaten. His last public speech was at Creggs in County Galway on Sunday 27 September, when, bareheaded in the rain, he repeated the by-now-old message, 'We shall continue this fight . . . We may not be able to gain it [Irish nationhood], but if not it will be left for those who come after us to win; but we will do our best.' The following Thursday he was back in his house at 9 Walsingham Terrace, Brighton, complaining of great pains – which he called rheumatism – in his arms. Katharine had to help him to bed and he was not able to rise. He stayed in bed over the weekend, feverish and in great pain, though he rallied sufficiently on the Sunday to sit up and smoke a cigar. The following Tuesday evening, 6 October 1891, he died in Katharine's arms. They had been married for 103 days.

Katharine bade him goodbye on the following Saturday; she had never visited her husband's homeland and it seemed inappropriate to do so now. The coffin reached Westland Row at 7.30 on the Sunday morning on a day of relentless rain, and great crowds followed it to St Michan's, where the first part of the funeral service was held. The coffin lay in state for some hours in City Hall before being taken for burial in the Catholic cemetery of Glasnevin. The rain had stopped, and as the October twilight came on the sky was clear enough for the thousands of mourners to note a brilliant bluish-white meteor searing across the sky – a fitting celestial mark of the end of a mythic champion. Maud Gonne, then twenty-six years old, told Yeats about it and he immortalised it in his late poem 'Parnell's Funeral'. It seemed to him a kind of completion that the tragic hero should be buried so close to the Great Comedian's tomb. Now, the simple granite boulder with the single word 'Parnell' upon it on the green plot so close to the soaring round tower are not inappropriate memorials to the two giants of nineteenth-century Irish history.

Parnell's death was sudden and unexpected, and even his adversaries mourned him. The *Times,* forgetting its old animosity towards him, called him 'one of the most remarkable figures of the century'. He was most keenly mourned by the rising Catholic bourgeoisie of the cities and larger towns, whom he had empowered and who now felt themselves able to make political judgements independently of their clergy. The grief – and the venom – his death evoked have been best typified in literature in the characters of Dante and Mr Casey in Joyce's *A Portrait of the Artist as a Young Man* (1916): the one categorising him as 'A traitor, an adulterer', the other collapsing in tears with 'Poor Parnell! My dead king!' and both showing equal amounts of hurt and disappointment. 'Ivy Day in the Committee Room', a story in *Dubliners* (1914) about a pro-Parnellite committee meeting to plan tactics for a municipal election long after the funeral, has a mock-heroic salute of ordnance to the dead king, as three bottles of stout placed on the hearth pop their corks.

It was difficult at the time for anyone to be impartial about Parnell's achievement; even now the high drama of his career and his disdain for the mores of the time make it hard to make a judgement on him. He is best seen as someone who carried on the work of O'Connell, whose even grander funeral took place when Parnell was eleven months old. He undoubtedly advanced the Irish cause in a way that caused few deaths or broken heads. His constitutionalism was built on his ability to use the threat of violence while ensuring that this threat did not break out in armed insurrection. He shared with O'Connell the sound conviction that a rising would hurt Ireland more than the perceived enemy. He must be given a great deal of the credit for settling the land question, though not quite in the way he would have wished. He knew that the Home Rule Bill of 1886 would not pass the Lords but he hoped that the next one would be advanced with such moral and political authority that even the upper house could not damn it without reason. His building up of the Irish Party into a disciplined political machine made obvious even to his enemies what

Ireland had known for a long time: that it was fit and ready for self-government and as dedicated to the principles of constitutional democracy as the Mother of Parliaments.

His greatest tactical fault was his refusal to engage with either authority or sympathy the million or more northern Protestants, upon whose atavistic fears the Tories could play so skilfully. Eighteen ninety-two could have been the year when the mettle of both sides might finally have been tested, but in the confusion after the Chief's fall there was no unity and no charismatic leader on the nationalist side. If Katharine had been single or a widow, if Parnell had refused to show any weakness in the face of O'Shea's early blackmail, if there had been enough money to buy her husband's silence, if his health had not been congenitally poor and sorely affected by the aftermath of the divorce case, if he had resigned, divorced and returned, as Rhodes had suggested . . . but then 'what if' in relation to history is the idlest of parlour games.

His embroilment with O'Shea showed him at his worst, but his passion for Katharine was such that it could at any time have won out against his political career. She lived on until 1921, her thirty years of widowhood dark with grief and mental breakdown. Her biography of her husband, which many think was adjusted by her first-born, Gerard O'Shea, to show his father in a kindlier light than it had originally, was published in two volumes in 1914, and it is still a significant document in terms of the information it contains about Parnell's private life, which was kept secret for so long. Parnell loved his country and Parnell loved his lass, and he thought he could give equal devotion to both. His personality remains the most enigmatic and engrossing of all those who over the centuries did what they could to sweeten Ireland's wrong, and he will continue to fascinate because of both his public and private careers.

SELECT BIBLIOGRAPHY

Bew, P. *C. S. Parnell*. Dublin, 1980.

Callaghan, M. R. *Kitty O'Shea*. London, 1989.

Connolly, S. J. *The Oxford Companion to Irish History*. Oxford, 1998.

Ervine, St J. *Parnell*. London, 1925.

Foster, R. *Modern Ireland 1600–1972*. London, 1988.

Kee, R. *The Green Flag*. London, 1972.

————. *The Laurel and the Ivy*. London, 1993.

Lee, J. *The Modernisation of Irish Society*. Dublin, 1973.

Lyons, F. S. L. *Charles Stewart Parnell*. London, 1977.

Lyons, J. B. *'What Did I Die Of?'* Dublin, 1991.

O'Shea, K. *Charles Stewart Parnell: His Love Story and Political Life*. London, 1914.

Vaughan, W. E., ed. *A New History of Ireland. Vol VI*. Oxford, 1996.